BYOB

BE YOUR OWN BANK

PERI SCOTT

Copyright © 2019 by Peri Scott

All rights reserved.

No part of this book may be reproduced in any form or by any electronic or mechanical means, including information storage and retrieval systems, without written permission from the author, except for the use of brief quotations in a book review.

❋ Created with Vellum

DISCLAIMER

This is a book about ideas. I am not a financial planner nor am I a tax expert. I have no qualifications in either of those fields, I am just an interested layperson. Please do not take the information in this book as financial advice or recommendations. Use the ideas in this book at your own discretion. All investing carries with it a certain amount of risk. I assume no responsibility nor liability for any financial gains or losses resulting from the implementation of my ideas. You are the one in control. That is the point.

CONTENTS

Introduction	xi
1. Philosophy	1
2. Margin	9
3. Dividends	13
4. The MACHINE	17
5. Cash Flow is KING	22
6. Possibilities	26
7. Math	31
8. Real Estate for the Rest of Us	37
9. Real Estate Pros & Cons	41
10. The Car Payment	44
Afterword	53
About the Author	55

To My Wife, Carol

You inspire me to be more everyday.

"Cash Flow is KING"
 -Danny Wong

INTRODUCTION

You can be your own banker.

You can have all of the power, all of the freedom and all of the control. You can be the master of your financial destiny.

No more sitting in your bankers office, hat in hand, waiting for them to tell you how much, if any, money they will lend to you at their preferred interest rate. No more wondering if you have enough assets, or too much "debt ratio" to get a loan. It is all you. You are the one deciding the interest rate, the payback schedule, the amount, and the risk tolerance.

Seem too good to be true?

It may seem that way, but when you follow my system, you become the proprietor of the golden rule:

"He who has the gold makes the rules"

I am not guaranteeing that you will become rich, nor am I guaranteeing that you will manage your newfound power responsibly. I hope you do, but what I am offering you is the ability to have the control. I am offering you a simple system

Introduction

where you are the one sitting behind the desk deciding if you are worthy. It is up to you.

I believe that money is a very useful tool. You can use this tool to build something, or you can send it to others foolishly. The difference between managing money wisely and being foolish with it comes down to a few things:

1. Math - If you actually do the math, you will often be surprised as to what makes the most sense; such as do I pay down my mortgage or invest in RRSPs? Doing the math sometimes reveals a path that is counterintuitive to what you thought was the best plan.
2. Philosophy - What are you actually trying to accomplish. Having "more money" is a pretty vague goal. You need to decide what you want money to do for you. Do you want to be free from a job you hate, or a tyrannical boss? Do you want to retire early and travel the world? Do you want to help out your destitute family members? Having a defined goal helps you to make better financial decisions, especially when you start to actually HAVE money.
3. Discipline - You need to make a plan and stick to it. Small refinements to optimize things are OK, but a well-executed financial plan requires consistency, thought and self-discipline. You need to commit to yourself and to your plan. You have to resist temptation. The latest 8K TV can wait.
4. Knowledge - This seems to be what everyone is looking for when they read a book like this. "Show me how". I love to learn new things, and

Introduction

the more you know the better. Please educate yourself as much as you can, as there are hundreds of great books, videos, podcasts, and seminars that will teach you about money, financial planning and investment strategies. I have spent years learning new ideas. Every time I learn something new I get excited. I can't wait to share it with my loved ones, and I feel empowered to take control of my financial life. As important as 'how' is, I believe that 'why' is equally as important. Knowledge of financial concepts and mindsets are often overlooked for "paint by numbers" approaches to building wealth creation systems.

5. Action - All of this knowledge is meaningless unless you take action. This has been said about a billion times by every motivational speaker of all time. It has been repeated so much because it is so true. Actually doing something, versus thinking about it, is life changing. Not only will you move forward, you learn things as you try new things. Reading about them is one form of learning, but actually doing things is a whole new world of education. You will see what actually works and doesn't work in the real world. You will have successes and failures. You will learn from all of it, and you will be better equipped to face these challenges in the future.

6. Mentoring - Get a mentor. The importance of this cannot be overstated. A mentor can save you a lifetime of pounding your head against a wall trying dumb ideas. Find someone who has done what you want to do and persuade them to take

Introduction

you under their wing. Do whatever you can to make it worth their while. Many accomplished people will admire you for your gumption, and agree to help you. This has also been suggested many times by many influencers and for good reason. It has tremendous value.

Thank you for picking up this book and being curious. I really hope it presents to you an idea that opens your eyes to new possibilities. My intention is that you find value in its pages and a new perspective in its message.

I often read books like this with a calculator in my hand, as I really like to see the math for myself. This often leads to a spreadsheet or two. Fill your boots. Feel free to take notes. I believe that by understanding and absorbing this philosophy you can apply the system to your own unique financial situation to build your fortune and prosper

1
PHILOSOPHY
BE IN CONTROL

THE KEY to success with this idea is knowing what you want. We want to be in control, and this is a way to be in control. You may trust and respect your banker, and that is your prerogative. By all means, continue your relationship with him/her if that makes you happy. I am just suggesting that there may be a different path for those of you who feel like you might be better off not begging for money from "The Man".

Being in control is the business that banks are in. That is great. Let's be friends and use the banks for our gain. We can all get along. We are going to create a great partnership. We are just going to use the system to benefit ourselves, whenever possible.

Often times, we look for information in books or on the Internet about "how" to do stuff. This is great, but it usually doesn't motivate us to take action unless we have a very clear and strong "why". I am not talking about some great desire to change the world, or a formal mission statement. I am talking about having defined objectives or goals that you want to accomplish, mostly in the form of financial goals or lifestyle objectives.

This could be as vague or silly as " I want to be stinking rich so I can impress everybody at the high school reunion". Not a great goal, but it is a good start. You would have to then break that down into specific and measurable units.

I.e. TEN million dollars in the bank

If you have a more realistic goal, such as "retire early" or "Extra income to buy some toys" then we are really getting somewhere. As you define your strategy, you need to figure out what it is you are trying to accomplish and then many of the decisions you make will conform to your end goal. None of this happens in a vacuum. We need to have a real life map.

What I am proposing here is really what I consider a financial foundation upon which to build the rest of your empire. There are many great ways to build wealth and I suggest you take advantage of as many as you can. Multiple streams of income is not just a cliché, it is really a great way to build wealth. I am a great admirer of ambitious people who pursue multiple income sources and I believe we live in a time and place where opportunities are abundant like never before in history. However, we need a place to start. We need to have a financial mechanism constructed that will provide us with the flexibility to chase after income opportunities while preserving and growing our nest egg.

This system is based upon a "workflow". We set up and control where the money comes from, where it goes, how much and when it all happens. We set strict rules and live by them. We exercise self-discipline and restraint. If it sounds boring and stuffy, I suppose it is. Most financial gurus suggest that getting rich SHOULD be boring. Get rich quick is a myth and is a very rare occurrence in the real world. Masters of money have usually been patient, meticulous and thoughtful. You will become a master of money. You will work your system like the "old money" oligarchs do. How much money you have to work with is absolutely irrelevant here. The system and the control is what is important, not the scale. I believe that the beauty of this system is that it is accessible to everyone, no matter how much they earn. If you have limited means, you will learn to manage your money like the wealthy. The principles are the same.

Creating your own bank is like sitting on the other side of the desk and making the calls. It is putting the power and the responsibility into your own hands. You are now the master of the vault. You can now enjoy the position of having it "both ways". A bank can take in 1 dollar and loan out several multiples of that dollar. This doesn't seem fair. It probably isn't, yet the banks can do it legally and ethically. This is their primary business. You are going to gain that same ability, only slightly modified.

The primary idea here that makes the whole system amazing is that we can borrow "money" from ourselves, without losing the income that the original money is making. It's like it was never gone. I know, this may seem strange. It is not how most people conceive of managing money.

I will offer an example of what I am talking about.

If you wanted to buy an item for $50, you might think about getting the item in one of TWO ways:

1. Save up $50 a little at a time
2. Buy the item on credit (borrow) and pay it back later.

This has been the time-honoured method for buying things and many people use (or overuse) the second option. Who saves up to buy a car these days?

Saving up money actually has diminishing returns.

Let's suppose you save up $50 by putting $10 a month into a savings account. It may earn you .01% interest by today's interest rates. If you take out that $50 to buy the item you want, you:

a. Have $0 left

b. Need to save up another $50

This can't even keep up with inflation, and you are theoretically losing money as you save it up. You are also wasting time and losing out on what is known as "opportunity cost".

If you buy the item on credit, you end up paying much more than the original cost of the item by adding interest to the final price. This is making someone else rich. Not a great scenario but it at least gets you your item right away.

There is actually a third option. This third option is what this book is all about.

This idea came from a pitch by some insurance companies I saw on the Internet. They claim you can borrow money from yourself, and keep the interest. You also keep your principle working for you the whole time. I thought to myself that sounded pretty cool. I wonder if there is a way to do this outside of an insurance policy. Since I was already investing in other things, I had the pieces of this puzzle already in front of me; I just had to put them together in the right way. None of these ideas are new and even the method is old hat for our friends the real estate investors.

Real estate investors have been doing this forever. They buy a property, rent it out and make payments for a while. The property sometimes goes up in value. They then refinance the property or take out a Home Equity Line of Credit (HELOC) against the equity in the home. Now they borrow money from the HELOC to buy another rental property, while still receiving rent payments on the entire property, without actually owning the whole thing (the bank still owns most of it). They are just slowly buying it back from the bank over time, using the rental income.

We are going to do the same thing, without having to buy a house. No need to save up thousands of dollars for a down payment. You can start with as little or as much as you like. It is leverage for everyone! Use the money you already have or can afford, and work the system as I explain it. Once you get the hang of it, you can increase the amount you contribute if you feel it is working. The important thing is the concept, not the scale. You being in control is what we are striving for. We can manage our "bank" like a real estate portfolio without the headaches of being a landlord. We can do it with money we already have, and we can leverage our assets on our own schedule.

So many investment decisions will be coming your way if you decide to create YourBank. In order to make these decisions easier, and to have a plan that works for you, you need to really spend the time thinking very hard about what your objectives are. You will need to decide if long-term growth is paramount, or if you are just saving to buy a ski-doo. You will also be choosing what to do with your dividends, and whether to reinvest, or spend. Depending on your endgame, how you construct the workflows within your banking empire is going to be very different. I will attempt to offer you the pros and cons of each type of strategy so that you will have enough information to construct your own banking system that works for you and your goals.

Once you have a meaningful goal set for yourself, you then build the machine and launch YourBank. As you grow, and as you learn more, you may want to readjust things. You may learn a better way to do things that further accelerates the plan. It is a layered approach. You will start with a foundation, and then add the workflows that keep the machine healthy, happy, and providing for you and your heirs. Welcome to high society.

In order to begin, we need to start somewhere, and that begins with finding a brokerage house that you can use to buy and sell stocks, transfer money to and from your other bank accounts, and set up your machine so that it all runs smoothly. Online and automatic are two things I would look for, as eventually, you will have other things to do besides playing with your money.

I am definitely not what you would call blue-blooded by any means. I came from humble beginnings, so I really can't speak to the veracity of what I am about to say. But from what I have gathered in my wanderings through life, it appears as though the super rich, "Old money" families do seem to have a philosophy that grows and preserves their wealth. They appear to place a very high regard for the family fortune as a unique and separate entity, apart from their own personal money. They become wards of the family fortune and contribute to it as a collective. It has been rumoured that they are allowed to borrow from the family, but have to pay it back with interest. They must share their knowledge with the other members of the family, and learn to benefit from the collective wisdom of the whole. All gains acquired through their individual endeavours must be funnelled back into the family fortune, which keeps it strong, powerful, and under family control. Occasionally, black-sheep members of the families break away from the collective, and try to go it alone, but generally they would be far better off continuing to be a part of the family dynasty and enjoying real wealth and power. "Many hands make light work", they say. I agree. Having this kind of family collective wealth would indeed be very powerful, but would require an uncommon degree of trust and loyalty to keep it intact.

One could adopt this philosophy amongst one's own trusted family members and it could potentially become a truly impressive fortune a lot quicker, but often times when it comes to money, people get a little crazy, and start to quibble about "fairness" and equitable effort levels. It might work if there is a very strong commitment from all parties involved to make the family bank the primary goal for everyone. There could be the potential for great strength, but it might require a lot of compromise. Not everyone is comfortable putting so much trust in others, or giving up control to other people with their own agendas. I am convinced, though, that if you could pull it off, you could reach financial independence incredibly fast, and have incredible strength if you have multiple like-minded people a part of one financial pool. One can dream...

If you cannot find additional family members to share in your vision that is perfectly OK. You can do this by yourself. If you have the same commitment to YourBank that the wealthy families of the world do to their family institutions, you should be able to reap the same rewards and enjoy the same feeling of power and control as them at a scale that suits you. You will make a promise to yourself to nurture YourBank with care and attention. You will find the self-discipline to build the machine in spite of temptations and distractions that beckon your money to lesser things. You will be patient, and let it bear fruit in the fullness of time and not give up at the first sign of adversity. You can do it. You can make the promise to yourself.

2

MARGIN
OTHER PEOPLE'S MONEY

THE KEY to success in this philosophy is having the ability to access cash, without having to beg for it. They way we will do that is through an investment vehicle called a Margin account.

Most brokerages offer this account type. You must apply for it, and you must have good credit to get one, but generally we want to be good financial citizens and have those types of things under control anyway, before we try to do any of this. If you do not have good-to-great credit, then I think maybe you need to get a few basic money management skills in place before you attempt this system.

Pay your bills.

Pay off your personal debts.

Pay on time.

There are many great books and advisors out there that offer fantastic advice on ways to get your act together, when it comes to debt and establishing good credit. Please take the time to figure this out. You will be doing yourself a great favour.

I have to assume that from this point forward, you are a

person that is at least able to qualify for a Line of Credit (LOC)

A margin account operates similar to a Line of Credit. The few differences here are:

1. The amount you can borrow depends of the value of the assets in the account
2. The amount you can borrow varies, depending on the daily fluctuations of the value of the assets in the account
3. If you continue to grow the assets, the amount you can borrow increases as well.

Item 1

As an example, if you have shares of a Blue chip company in your portfolio, the amount the brokerage may agree to lend you could be as high at 70% of the value of the shares. So if you have $1000 worth of shares of XYZ company, and the brokerage thinks that this company is A-OK then you can borrow up to $700. Pretty cool!

Item 2

If the value of your shares in XYZ company fall by 25%, the amount you can borrow becomes 70% of the new value ($750) so the new amount you can borrow is $525. This is a fact I need you to really wrap your head around, as it is very important later on.

Item 3

If your shares go UP by 25% then the amount you can borrow goes up as well. The new value of your shares is $1250.00 and you can now borrow up to $875. This also applies if you buy more shares as well. You, once again, have some control over your borrowing limit.

In order to use a margin account wisely, you must understand not only its benefits, but also its risks. As with any type of investments and money vehicles, there is always some risk involved, and there is always some form of risk management that you can employ.

Every stock has its own perceived value in the eyes of the brokerage, so every position you carry will have its own risk factor. The brokerage may lend you 70% on some stocks, and 50% on others. They may only lend you 25% or NOTHING on some stocks. It is important to do your research and figure out what that perception is, before you choose to invest in any particular investment. Also, to make matters more complicated, some brokerages change their minds EVERY DAY. You never know what the amount could be tomorrow. Keep this in mind when you are designing your strategy. Of course, the account will always show you the current status of your margin, and will let you know how much you have left to borrow that day. I like the idea of having a very few, well-researched companies in my account, in order to minimize the craziness of a volatile market, or a skittish broker. This way, I can feel a little more certain about the future status of my credit line.

Of course, this ability to borrow money comes with the universal obligation that accompanies most lending vehicles... interest.

Yes, most brokerages will charge you interest on any money you borrow from the margin account. Why wouldn't they? There has to be something in it for them, other wise why offer the account in the first place. Generally, the brokerage will charge you interest monthly, and the money can come from your margin account, or any account you choose. The interest rates vary, but usually are not unreasonable. In my experience the interest rates are usually not as good a HELOC but not as bad as an unsecured loan.

We are not completely eliminating banks, we are just using them differently, and paying interest is no exception. Of course, we hope the benefits of borrowing the money (i.e. Investing it) will make up for the interest we are charged. I will discuss some strategies later in this book to address this charge.

3

DIVIDENDS

FREE MONEY

My preferred method of growing my wealth is to use dividends for monthly cash flow.

When you buy shares of a company, you are essentially becoming a part owner of that company. As part owner, you are sometimes entitled to share in the profits of that company and many companies offer this distribution monthly or quarterly.

When researching a company look for:

1. Dividends that have been ongoing for many years
2. Dividends that have increased regularly over time
3. A return on investment (called the yield) that meets your requirements

For example, Bank of Nova Scotia (BNS) has been paying dividends for over a century and has consistently increased the payout for years. This would be a safe bet. Many bank stocks offer a similar situation, with a trade-off being that the yield is a conservative 3% or so. Depending on your risk tolerance, you may or may not decide to invest part of your portfolio in ultra-conservative companies and just work the machine. That is a perfectly legitimate way to fund the system to your benefit.

Inversely, many companies offer super-high yields like 11% or 12% or higher, but I would be cautious as to the long-term sustainability of that payout, and even the company. These are often a short term spike due to the price of the stock dropping, which sometimes leads to the dividend being re-adjusted, or eliminated.

In order to calculate the yield, just add the dividends up over a year and divide by the price of the stock. Let's look at a detailed quote for the Bank of Nova Scotia:

Quarterly Dividend per share: $0.850

$0.850 x 4=$3.40 Per year

Share Price: $75.52

Yield: $3.40 / 75.52 = 0.045 or 4.5% yield

This number is usually indicated when you research a stock. Usually the yield will be calculated based on two things, the closing price as of yesterday, and the sum of the dividends in the trailing 12 months. As dividend payouts change this can sometimes be a little misleading, so it is usually helpful to do your own calculation based on the current dividend payout and the current stock price, as that will equal your actual ROI or yield.

Most people prefer a mix of high and low yield paying companies as you can set an average that makes sense for you. As they raise or lower their payouts, you can rebalance your holdings to keep the average yield acceptable to you. There are so many possibilities, and you can mix and match in a million different ways. As you become more familiar with this process and the companies that you are investing in, you may grow to be more aggressive as sometimes risk is only as high as your knowledge level. Some sophisticated investors appear like they are taking huge risks, but are actually in control due to having understood the market, the companies they are investing in, and risk mitigation processes.

I really like companies that distribute their dividend monthly, rather than quarterly, as it makes budgeting easier. Most people manage their money on a monthly basis, and I am no exception. I can plan for money movement and set automated contributions if I have a monthly income. I also like the feeling of seeing money coming in every month. It makes me feel good about the plan, and it keeps me excited and motivated to keep working the plan. Quarterly dividends are Ok, but they don't really have the same impact as monthly, unless they are quite substantial. It really does give the appearance of an "income" when you are receiving them monthly. Don't skip out on a quarterly dividend if it meets your criteria, by all means. I am always OK with making passive income, however it comes my way. If you have a mix of monthly and quarterly dividends in your portfolio then it really doesn't matter, you will see income coming into your account all the time, and it will fire you up when you get the quarterly "bonus". It all depends on how you look at it.

The other cool thing about good quality dividend paying companies is they often raise their dividend. This is like getting a raise! You are humming along happily receiving your dividend income while planning your future when "BAM!" You get a bump in your monthly income. You received a raise without even asking for one or doing any extra work. You received a bump in your monthly salary by just being a cool guy. Now THAT is my kind of compensation package.

If you bought a stock a certain price and the dividend is a certain price, you are enjoying a specific yield on your investment. When they raise the dividend, you are now receiving a higher yield than you were before on the money that you had previously invested. Nice. Your return on investment (ROI) has gone up. That is always a morale booster.

There are two things I really love about dividends.

1. They just keep coming.

-If you invest in the right companies, you will keep receiving money from them basically FOREVER. You never have to lift a finger and you get paid. Passive income!

2. They are Tax friendly

-Here in Canada, dividends are taxed at a very favourable rate. Revenue Canada accepts that eligible dividends are "after tax" dollars as the corporation that distributes them has already paid taxes on that money. You will only pay the difference between the corporate tax rate, and your personal tax rate. (Please refer to a tax professional for more information)

Now here is what to do with your dividends...

4

THE MACHINE

PUT YOUR MONEY TO WORK

OK

Now that we have the parts established, let's build the MACHINE!

We want to use this process to build our wealth, and provide a mechanism to fund our cash flow needs for the foreseeable future. We want control of how much and when, and we want to automate as much as possible so we can focus on other things.

The key principle here is to make your "bank" the centre of your universe. All initiatives involving money from now forward will all be funnelled through the "bank". For simplicity sake, let's call it "*YourBank*".

YourBank, being a bank, is now in the business of financing your life. If you need a loan, for any reason, you go to YourBank. If you need to direct money towards a goal, you go to YourBank. This is its primary reason for existing. To help you reach your financial goals.

Of course, YourBank must act like a proper bank, and do its due diligence concerning any possible money lending that it does. If you are to get the most out of this, you must have strict criteria that you refuse to compromise, in order to keep YourBank healthy and making profit. This means:

1. Assessing risk
2. Make sure all loans are very likely to be paid back in full, in the allotted timeframe
3. Make sure all loans are leveraged appropriately
4. Make sure it is always profitable
5. Be a well run business
6. Keep great records
7. Get advice from experts
8. Manage your money

The first thing you need to do is devote yourself to the establishment of YourBank. In real terms, this means decide upon a fixed amount of your current income that you are going to automatically deposit into YourBank every paycheque. This is the most important step, and the foundation upon which all additional components stand. You MUST commit to this, and you MUST not waiver. EVER. This is the family bank. It is the patriarch of your life. Make sure the amount you commit hurts. If it doesn't hurt a little, it is not enough to really make this work. Remember, this is a new mindset, and it will take a little getting used to.

This is the "pay yourself first" mindset on steroids. You must automate this contribution, and you must commit to living off of the remaining money every month. It may be hard at first, but you will adapt and figure out how to live happily on much less than you did before. Living frugally is cool these days, I hear.

Every time you deposit your monthly contribution to the

family fortune, you buy shares of your favourite dividend producing stock(s). Always. ALL CONTRIBUTIONS MUST BUY MORE STOCK. No exceptions. This rule needs to be unbreakable. This is a set it and forget it type of thing, and you will commit to this for the rest of your life. This is the beating heart of the machine.

As your portfolio grows, the amount you can borrow grows as well. If you continue to contribute and buy shares, the amount you can borrow constantly goes up, and the amount of dividends grows as well. So over time your bank becomes more and more powerful, as it compounds its leverage.

At first, if you have accumulated $10,000.00 in Your-Bank, and you need $2500 for something, this is 25% of the holdings, and may feel a little scary borrowing that much. As the portfolio grows, borrowing $2500 will seem insignificant as it becomes less and less of the total margin available. This makes sense of course, but the interesting part is as the dividends grow, the payback time accelerates as well. Your dividends will pay back any loans all by themselves, so the bank's exposure is minimized. Of course, you, the client, must pay back ALL of the $2500 you borrowed, (Maybe even with interest, if you really want to be like a banker) so the bank makes money on the transaction.

Remember, the monthly contribution does NOT represent loan payback. All money borrowed from the bank must be paid back, in full, ***IN ADDITION TO*** the monthly contribution. This ensures the health of the bank. We are always concerned about the health of the bank, as this is your family fortune, and is sacred. If you continue to hold true to this idea, YourBank will take care of you and your heirs for a long, long time. I think this is what they call "old money".

An example of using this system in real life would be if

you wanted to buy a rental property. You would borrow your down payment from YourBank and get a mortgage from a traditional bank. You then buy your rental property and rent it out, hopefully making enough to cover your mortgage and pay back the down payment. Any profit you make from the remaining money will have the appropriate portion added to the monthly contribution. You personally have profited, and so has YourBank, as you are forever beholden to your patriarch.

Of course, you are free to use this any way you please. I am merely offering a philosophy that I feel is designed to keep you accountable. Since you own the bank, everybody wins, but the underlying authority of YourBank keeps the machine running smoothly. As soon as you become undisciplined with your own rules, you will have a hard time managing things. We will come to depend on the bank to take care of us, so it needs to be strong and powerful. Yet it is also benevolent, as it is always happy to give you a loan and it exists solely for your benefit. It has no other customers, so it always has time for you.

As long as you try to keep your lending maximum to an amount that won't trigger a margin call if the stock market crashes, you should be fine. Investing in paper assets always comes with its fair share of risk, but managing risk is part of being in business and part of being an investor. Use your discretion, and set yourself up for success.

Part of this mindset is now thinking of the bank, every time you need money for things outside of your everyday expenses. You should have a budget, and live within it. You should be paying yourself (YourBank) first, and living on the remainder. Your monthly budget should include your normal everyday living expenses and not much else.

In the event that things come up that are outside of your

ordinary expenses (investment opportunities, tax bills, car repairs, car replacements, home repairs, etc.<—you decide) this is when you turn to YourBank. You are borrowing from yourself, to help yourself, and paying yourself back, to allow yourself to help yourself again in the future. It's all you, baby!

Instead of thinking, "Can I afford this?" start thinking, "How much do I need to contribute to my bank to generate enough income to pay for this?" or "Can the bank cover this loan?" If the bank can't afford it, neither can you. Don't do it. You are now only as rich as YourBank is. This will keep you committed to growing YourBank and keeping your spending on the straight and narrow. It requires self-discipline, but it is much easier to manifest self-control when it benefits mostly YOU.

5

CASH FLOW IS KING

MORE MONEY IS USUALLY THE SOLUTION

Y<small>OU HEARD THAT RIGHT</small>. Cash flow is KING. Now you may be thinking that this system really doesn't focus on cash flow, it is more about growing your net worth. True. I want you to use this system to build yourself a foundation upon which to pursue cash flowing opportunities.

-Borrow from yourself to buy a rental property
-Borrow from yourself to invest in the stock market
-Borrow from yourself to invest in a business
-Borrow from yourself to pay down debt

Most investors and money-savvy people use credit (read: leverage) to accelerate their path to financial freedom. Unless you earn an extremely high income, it is very difficult to build substantial wealth without using other people's money. Real estate investors know this. They can put a relatively small deposit on a rental property (5-25%) and use the bank money for the rest. They use the rental income (also other peoples money) to pay the mortgage. This is called leverage. Why not use your OWN money for leverage?

1. You don't have to ask for it, you just take it
2. You can pay it back on your own schedule
3. YourBank increases your net worth, which banks LOVE
4. Your monthly dividends add to your income, which banks LOVE
5. You set the interest rate on any loans (if any)
6. It is a safety net in case any of your ventures turn sour

I believe if you are seriously pursuing financial independence, you should be acquiring cash-flow producing assets. Period. After financing YourBank, this should be your focus. In fact, I would suggest that YourBank's primary purpose is to fund your investment ideas. Investing in anything that creates cash flow is going to be easier, less risky and, frankly, less scary if you have the family fortune to fall back on. This is often overlooked. I say, "Go for it" when it comes to finding ways to earn more income. I just think having old money backing your endeavours is a pretty nice cushion to help you chase your cash flow dreams with just a little bit more enthusiasm.

YourBank has the appearance of a "nest egg", and I suppose it is, but you are using this nest egg as a tool. You are actually leveraging this wealth to grow your income. You are financing your dreams. You are jumping on opportunities as they arise. It would sure be nice to be prepared when cash flow opportunities appear out of nowhere, as they often do. Having YourBank up and running will give you that ability. As they say, "Luck" is when opportunity meets preparation. Be prepared with YourBank.

Some people use their primary residence as a bank. They take out HELOCs and use that money to invest. That is a great idea. The interest rates are usually quite good, and you don't have to ask for money once it is set up. The advantage to our plan is that you are borrowing against an asset that is still making money. If done right, the assets in your portfolio will pay for any interest charges you may incur, and maybe even extra. As long as your regular contributions continue religiously (just as you promised the stern-faced board of directors of the bank {YOU} that they would) your "nest egg" is working triple duty. It is growing your net worth, providing for your future, and working hard to increase your cash flow NOW! I LOVE IT!

Which cash flow ideas you entertain is up to you. There are many out there:

1. Real Estate
2. Flipping
3. Rentals
4. REITs
5. Dividend paying stocks or funds
6. Private equity investing
7. Running your own business
8. Royalties
9. E-commerce
10. Blogging
11. YouTube

The possibilities are endless. You can easily research these vehicles through books, videos, the Internet and seminars.

BYOB

There are really a ton of great ideas out there for making money, and I have experimented with many of them. Once you find a cash flow producing mechanism that you like and understand, you can now use YourBank to fund it. It really is a win-win scenario. YourBank wins and so do you!

6

POSSIBILITIES

COMPOUNDING

We all know that compounding is a magical thing. It is how we can turn a little money into a lot. So in the context of our system, does it make sense to:

1. Reinvest our dividends
2. Borrow to reinvest
3. Withdraw

Here is where math can help, but you really have to know what your objectives are. Managing the cash flow always comes down to whether you want the money now or later. It also depends on whether you have other things going on.

Reinvest dividends

In the scenario where you reinvest your dividends, you are treating your portfolio like a DRIP (Dividend Re-investment

Plan). This helps you grow your holdings faster, but doesn't really help with cash flow. So you need to decide which is more important to you. Maybe when you first get started, you may want to reinvest your dividends, as you want to get that nest egg built up so you can start to leverage it. That would be a good plan, as you really aren't making that much off of the dividends anyway, and you can't really borrow that much either. The initial growth of the bank is from your monthly contributions to begin with, so every little but extra will help. But again it's up to you.

Borrow to invest

One way to grow your portfolio is to use the margin to buy more stocks. If you do that, you a really mimicking real estate in that you can own assets without actually paying for them yet. This is interesting in two ways:

Let's assume BNS again:

1. You can buy $1000 worth of stock for $250 (fully leveraged)
2. You will collect dividends on $1000 worth of stock.

Now you are making more money right away, instead of waiting until you have accumulated $1000 worth of stock. Of course, you will be paying interest on the $750 you owe, but if you manage the ratios of margin and equity, you can often times completely pay for the interest with dividends. Generally, look for a dividend yield that is a higher percentage than the interest rate. This is like an interest free loan. (I know, technically you are still paying for it, as the dividends are also your money - but you didn't trade your *time for it*)

You now have some choices. This is where your philosophy comes in.

1. You can pay back the $750 with dividends
2. You can pay back the $750 with your contributions
3. You continue to buy stock with your contributions, thus lowering your margin rate and increasing your dividends
4. Reinvest the dividends and never pay back the $750, as over time it will become insignificant
5. Pay back the $750 like a separate loan, with money that is not a part of your contribution, and let the banks continue to profit. (You can even pay it back with interest, if you want to be a scoundrel)

As you can see there are many ways to manage this. This is why your philosophy is so important, otherwise you will constantly have to make decisions about what to do every month. Have a set plan and stick to it. This will help the machine work smoothly, and have a predictable tempo. When you know that monthly cash flow is king, for example, the way you manage dividends and loan payback becomes a lot clearer.

If we stick to the philosophy of keeping YourBank front and centre in our life, we should really decide to keep the percentage of income we invest back into the bank the same. So if we are currently contributing 10% of our after-tax income to the family fortune, then if we receive $100 in dividends in a month, we really should be keeping that ratio intact and contributing $10 of the $100 to the plan. This keeps us focused on the final objective while still letting us mix and match how we distribute our extra income. This also increases our contributions in step with our income growth and accelerates our plan towards financial independence. This is compounding at it's finest.

If you were to model your workflows after our imaginary wealthy aristocrats, we would set up our system like a true family fortune. We would set up the margin account, invest in really good dividend paying stocks and have all parties involved contribute as much as they can from their personal income.

Then, when the bank is sufficiently funded, we would loan money from the bank to each member with a strict payback covenant that shall not be broken. Each member would take their loaned money and invest in their own moneymaking endeavours. Hopefully, they will each be successful and earn a decent profit with their investment. Now they will pay back their loan (with interest) to the bank, and increase their monthly contribution to the bank with the profits from their outside investment.

Once the loan is paid back in full, they are free to borrow some more money to continue to invest outside of the bank. Since they are paid in full, and their contributions have increased, they can now borrow even more money from the bank, as there is more money to borrow, and they have a proven track record. Win/Win, once again. The bank has prospered, and so has its benefactors.

This model covers most of our philosophical tenets. We are growing and caring for our bank. We are leveraging our participation in the bank. We are increasing our monthly cash flow via investing the bank's money in income producing assets, and we are finally re-investing the spoils of our efforts back into the bank. We are creating a dynasty. We can also take what we have learned and share it among our other members in order to help them be successful and that, in turn, helps the bank be successful, thus, perpetuating the system and the family fortune.

I recently asked my wife if she had two choices which would she choose:

1. Someone pays off all of your debt for you. You are now debt free.
2. Someone gives you the equivalent amount of your debt in cash.

She instantly said she would rather have the money in cash. She could instantly see that building your fortune is a much more compelling goal than paying off your debts. If you can increase your monthly income, you are always going to be in a far more powerful position than you were before. You now have the means to pay down your debt if you choose. You now have the freedom to maybe choose a different career. If you are debt free, sure you have some extra cash flow, but you are still trading your time for money. You still have to go to work everyday to invest that extra cash. Not the worst thing in the world, but I know that I would like to have more choices than that. I would like to be able to spend my time as I choose. My time is the most valuable thing I have. If I have multiple streams of income, and a large family fortune, my life is my own. I am in control of my time. Keeping my focus on strengthening the foundation of YourBank gives me back my time. It gives me a feeling of self-efficacy that can sometimes be hard to find in this modern world.

7

MATH

THE UNIVERSAL LANGUAGE

LET'S look at some charts. Math will always tell us the truth, whether we like it or not.

We should make the most of our financial decisions from the numbers. Often the truth is counterintuitive and we need it shown to us in black and white in order for us to be convinced of the right thing to do. Of course, this isn't always the way to go, as the whole point of this is to make your life the way you want it. What might be important to one person isn't necessarily important to another person. You get to decide. That is the point of this machine- for you to have choices. When you have math to show you the way, it makes a lot of decisions easier. Sometimes clarity is found in numbers, then your emotions will follow suit.

Leverage

In order to be responsible with our bank, and try to be appropriately crotchety, we will always have a thorough understanding of the risk involved in loaning money to ourselves. The first thing we need to determine, and keep a running account of, is how much we can reasonably loan out at any given time. This will be an outcome of math and your risk tolerance. We mentioned this before, but just to illustrate:

Let's assume we have a portfolio of 1 stock, worth $1000. The brokerage agrees to lend us up to 50% of the value of the stock.

Stock value: $1000
　　Margin: $500
　　We can borrow *up to* $500

This scenario leverages us to our maximum. Now being bankers, we need to determine if we want to expose the bank to this kind of risk, as the market could fluctuate and the value of our portfolio could go down, thus leaving us facing a margin call. I don't know any bankers who would agree to this.

Stock value falls to $950
　　Margin: $450
　　We now owe the brokerage $50. Due TODAY.

That is no fun.

So if I were a typical stuffy banker, I would plan for the worse case scenario. If we look at the stock market historically, harsh bear markets tend to happen pretty quickly

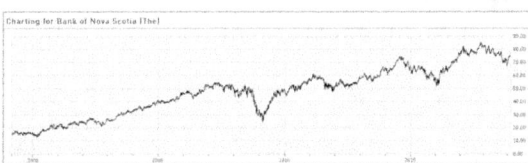

Bank of Nova Scotia Chart

This is a price chart for Bank of Nova Scotia (one of my favourite Blue chip stocks). If you look at the infamous 2008 market crash, the price dropped from roughly $53 to roughly $25 (About a 52% decline). This would hurt us badly if we had been over leveraged.

Stock price before: $53.00
　　Margin: $39.75

Stock price after: $25
　　Margin: $18.75

Here, we even assume that the broker is going to keep a 70% margin on this stock. During a bear market, they may get a little skittish, and reduce the margin rate. You never know.

So if I we want to protect ourselves from these types of events, It would make good sense to limit our margin "loan" limit to 50% of the allowable margin.

. . .

Stock price: $53.00
   Margin: 39.75
   YourBank credit limit: $18.75

This does not eliminate risk but it definitely mitigates it. Your risk tolerance may differ, and that is completely up to you, but I, personally, like to sleep at night. So I keep my bank's lending limits conservative. After all, the health and welfare of *YourBank* comes first, right? An additional bonus to being conservative is that it may keep you from borrowing more than you can reasonably pay back, as we want to keep loan repayments and monthly contributions separate. The banks always look at your debt ratio, and so should you.

Another good reason to have a conservative credit limit is that it makes it easier for YourBank to cover any loans that you may "default on". If you have a $100,000.00 portfolio and you borrow $5000, the dividends from your 100K can pay back the loan pretty quickly even if you can't. This protects YourBank from you being a deadbeat.

Portfolio: $100,000.00

Yearly Dividend (5% Yield): $5000

YourBank can pay back the $5000 within a year from dividends alone, (not including interest & taxes), so you can take your sweet time paying back the bank. As always, the family bank must always be healthy if it is to be able to take care of the family fortune for you.

Insurance

Since we are stealing ideas from Real estate investors, let's keep rolling along with that theme. If you were a real estate investor and you bought a property to rent, one of the things I hope you would do is buy insurance. I would hate to see your hard earned capital go up in smoke in the event of a fire, or a flood. Most rational people buy insurance on all of their assets. It is the smart thing to do. You can get insurance on houses, cars, paintings, jewelry, etc. You can even get "insurance" on stocks. Here is how.

Options

If you open a margin account at most brokerages you can also apply for the ability to trade options. Options trading is a book all to itself, and I will not get into that here, but there is one particular options transaction that you can use to protect your holdings against a catastrophic market crash.

Options are exactly what they sound like. You can buy or sell the "option" to buy or sell a particular stock at a later date. This can get quite convoluted if you explore all of the permutations, and there are a lot of really good books about how to use options to grow your wealth. We will try to keep things simple here, and discuss the mechanics of how to use options as insurance.

You can decide how much you want to spend and how much you are willing to lose. The more you are willing to let the price drop, the cheaper the options become. So if you have a stock that is trading at $25 today and you want to insure it will still be worth $25 in the future, you buy the option to sell your shares at $25 in 6 months. This is named a "Call". This "contract" obligates someone to buy your shares at your whim on or before the agreed date at the agreed price. This will cost you a premium; maybe a few cents per share, depending on the stock. Options are sold in batches of 100, so you are making an agreement on 100 shares at a time. If the stock price goes down to $15 you can now exercise your option to sell your shares at $25. Pretty cool. You have now saved your fortune from collapse. If the stock price goes from $25 to $50, then you would just not exercise your option and it will expire worthless. No harm done, and you can chalk up the cost of the options as your insurance premium.

If you think that you can tolerate a certain drop in price, you can buy options to sell at $20, so if the price goes down to $10 again, you can sell at $20. You will still have preserved a little wealth, and you can buy the shares right back at $10 and double your dividends. Sweet! The reason you may want to lower your strike price is these options are usually cheaper, and you may have a limit to how much you want to spend in order to preserve your gains.

8

REAL ESTATE FOR THE REST OF US
THE BASICS

Real Estate Fundamentals

THERE ARE many ways to invest in real estate. I am sure there are many that I am not even aware of, but we will talk about two types here and discuss the basic mechanisms for both styles. Real estate is a great way to invest and grow your money, and it has been around for a long time. The underlying principles of real estate investing are straightforward most of the time, and you can read about them in many books. I am going to present a different approach to this system so I want to explain the fundamentals first.

Some people buy properties, fix them up, and then sell them for a profit. This is called house flipping and can be quite profitable if you know what you are doing. It is very market specific and is an awful lot of work. We wont be discussing this method.

Some people use a buy and hold strategy. They buy a property, and then rent it out. There are several permutations to this strategy, but the basic math is:

If the rent you charge a tenant can pay off the mortgage

and the expenses on the property, while leaving a profit every month, then it is a good investment. This is the end game and it can be a bit of a challenge to find a property that meets all of the criteria. However, it has been a great way to build wealth for a long time and will continue to do so.

If I break down the steps to becoming rich using buy and hold real estate, it is pretty close to the following:

1. Save up a down payment. In Canada, the banks require a 25% down payment for rental properties

2. Look for a property that you can afford
3. Look for a property that you can rent out at a rate high enough to pay off the mortgage and expenses - lots of math
4. Negotiate the price of the house
5. Buy the house
-Realtor fees
-Lawyers' fees
-Title transfer fees
-Property taxes
-Utility hookups
-Bank fees
-Mortgage negotiations
-Credit checks
6. Take possession of the house
7. Fix up house nice enough to be a desirable rental
8. Advertise for a tenant
9. Screen tenants
10. Choose tenant
11. Address any maintenance concerns for the tenant
12. Collect damage deposit

13. Create or commission rental agreement
14. Start collecting rent
15. Wait for the house to go up in value as per the local market (cross fingers)
16. Pay down mortgage
17. When there is enough equity in the home, go to bank
18. Ask for a Home Equity Line of Credit on the rental property
Or
18a. Ask to refinance rental property
19. Get HELOC or New mortgage
20. Use newfound money to buy new rental property
21. Look for property...

As you can see there is a process. I have stated that the process has been written about in hundreds, if not thousands, of books for a long time and you can find information about it just about anywhere. Don't get me wrong; this is a great way to build wealth. It just requires a lot of time, money, patience, know-how, and luck.

Leverage

The best part of real estate investing is the use of leverage or Other Peoples Money. You can pay a small percentage of the total value of the property as a down payment and still receive rent or income on the full value of the property. Cool!

You then have the tenant(s) pay your mortgage for you (OPM) and then you can borrow against the equity in the property to buy the next property. If you continue to leverage in this way, your wealth will build exponentially as each time you do this it doubles your rate of return. More and more tenants are repaying the money you borrow, so you dig yourself out of debt faster and faster. This is the beauty of real estate and the leverage available to you in that space. This is compounding at its finest.

9

REAL ESTATE PROS & CONS
STEALING THE MODEL

So we know that real estate investing is awesome in its ability to leverage debt and use other people's money. It works for many reasons but is not without its downside; the biggest of which is that it usually takes quite a bit of money to get into.

What if we were to use many of the principles of real estate investing and applied them to YourBank? We could have most of the benefits with very few of the detriments.

Here we go...

Down Payment

With your margin account you could buy a blue chip stock (House) with as little as 30% down. Not that I would suggest you maximize your margin this much, but you can see how you can get a lot of stocks for your money if you leverage. One thing you can do with your margin account is NOT leverage. You can buy stocks with cash. I am not sure you can do that with real estate unless you have an awful lot of money. You can leverage as much or as little as you like. You have total freedom here.

House Price

With YourBank, you decide how expensive the "house" you buy is. You can start with $100 and still make the math work! It's awesome to be able to manipulate the whole deal at your leisure. You are able to scale the transaction to fit your current wealth situation. You are not limited to your current "Market price" in your area. You can decide how much you want to pay and then you pay it. As long as you leverage appropriately, you will always make money from your dividends. Only have $50? No problem! You can start right away, and receive your first dividend in about a month. It is custom built just for you.

Rent

With good dividend paying stocks, your "renter" will pay you every month or quarter like clockwork, and will rarely be late, rarely miss a payment, and occasionally will voluntarily raise the rent. They will take care of the "house" for you, and will not demand you fix a toilet. They will not destroy your property. They will leave the place clean. They will be non-smokers and have no pets. They will shovel the walk and cut the lawn. They will be perfect and you will never have to speak to them. They will probably rent the place FOREVER.

Leverage

When you want to use the "house" to buy another

"house" you have many options. You can borrow against the value of the "house" and buy another "house" (stock). You can add value to the current "house" by buying more of that "house" (stock). You can split the difference. You can sell a little bit of one house to buy another. You can borrow against the value of the house to buy more of that same house. The possibilities are endless, and you never have to ask permission. You can just do it. You can set it up so that the math works every time. You borrow or invest as much as the "rent" can handle. If you buy more "house" the rent automatically goes up.

You can even have some fun and treat each individual stock as a separate "rental property" and treat them as such. You follow the standard real estate mechanisms of leverage and rent and you can grow your fortune through intelligent use of leverage and cash flow producing assets.

Cash flowing assets can be rental properties, businesses, e-commerce websites, or many other things. They are all great, and most wealthy people have more than one of these as it is very prudent to have multiple streams of income, and hedge your bets against any one of them failing.

Using YourBank to finance these endeavours is the perfect way to have your money working for you twice, and growing your family fortune exponentially.

So you can actually have a REAL house as part of the family fortune. Or you can own a business. They can all be funded by the bank, and have their proceeds feed directly back into the machine.

10

THE CAR PAYMENT

USING YOURBANK IN THE REAL WORLD

So there I was, all proud of myself, having thought up this great idea for YourBank. I explain it to my wife and my kids. I excitedly describe its merits to some of my friends. They all think its great. I am a hero.

Now it comes down to reality.

"OK, genius" said the love of my life.

"I want a new car. How is the bank going to buy me one?"

"Well, there are a few ways we can go..." I replied.

"Well, what is the *best* way?" she insisted.

"Um... I'm not sure. Let me do some math".

30 or 40 spreadsheets later I think I have the answer. I excitedly explain the method we will use to buy a new car AND keep growing our fortune. I show her the math.

"Humph" she says, fancy financial calculator in hand.

I should mention here that my spouse is one of the smartest people I know and that she also works in the financial business and is an expert at financial math.

Tough crowd, I know.

"Why don't you do it this way?" she says, as she grabs a piece of paper and a pen and starts to scribble furiously.

I counter with "OK that works, but we are paying too much interest that way."

15 more spreadsheets.

"I think I have it!" I shout triumphantly.

We go over the numbers again. This version seems to make a lot of sense.

Plan #63a

Set a periodic contribution to the margin account. DO NOT DEVIATE!

Buy dividend-paying shares every month with contribution money.

Now set a FIXED amount (equal to car payment) to borrow from margin account to be automatically transferred to the car payment account every month. In this way, we are amortizing the car loan to our selves from the "bank".

This method increases the amount of money owing in the margin account every month until the dividends grow enough to cover the car payment. Then, as the dividends grow even more, they start to pay down the margin balance as well. The key to this is the continuation of the stock purchases every month. The margin balance creates a nice curve.

This creates a nice, predictable cash workflow that we can track and control. The best part is, the bank is paying for my new car, not me. This is the dream.

Think bigger

We were excited about our new plan. We were going to be able to have it both ways:

We were simultaneously growing our wealth, while buying a new car with money that I didn't trade my time for. Life was good!

There are many ways to structure these deals, but this one made sense for our lifestyle. We wanted to know how much we were going to spend every month.

I happened to be perusing one of my favourite bloggers sites, when I was intrigued by a graph that he presented. It was a formula that indicated how quickly you could retire vs. what percentage of your income you invested. The higher the percentage, the quicker you could retire and it seems to be exponential, not linear.

I lamented to myself that I wish I could afford to invest a higher percentage of my income into the "bank". That would be great.

Then our car payment plan popped into view.

"What a minute!"

"What if, instead of buying just a car with this plan, we bought our WHOLE LIFE?"

I frantically ran spreadsheet after spreadsheet to see if the math would work.

It did.

I calculated that if we invested EVERY DOLLAR WE MADE into the margin account, then withdrew what we needed for monthly expenses each month, we could accelerate the growth of our dividends by gigantic proportions. We would be having it both ways at the grandest scale possible!

Spreadsheet after spreadsheet was painstakingly created to show every possible margin ratio, every possible stock market crash, and every possible unexpected expense. It even included a car payment. It all worked out.

If we limited our monthly withdrawal to the correct amount, we would be financially free in 8 years. I was flabbergasted. I never thought it could be possible. But there it was, right in front of me. The math didn't lie.

I calculated different exit strategies at different times. We could wait until the dividends paid off the margin balance, or we could sell enough stock to bring the margin owing to zero or somewhere in between.

Suddenly we could control when we retired and how rich we wanted to be when we did. It was all there in black and white, and I was the master of it.

Mind Set

I realize that there is a more tax efficient way to do this. Just contribute as much as you can afford and then leverage within the margin account to match what you make in a month. That way the interest is a tax write off. If you are a keener, that is way to do it. Keep the ratios the same as they would be if you invested it all then withdrew your monthly expenses.

We have to keep in mind human nature. We are designed as Homo sapiens to survive. It is our greatest instinct. We are much more motivated to avoid pain than we are to seek pleasure. We are always reluctant to do anything that feels like we are taking money away from ourselves.

This would apply to the concept of contributions to our fortune, where we would take away money from our checking account and put it into an investment. Since we are surviving on the money in that account, removing it actually feels unsafe, or dangerous, so we will tend to contribute a "safe" amount. An amount we feel we can live without. It actually feels like we are losing that money because that is where our "stash" is. It is our life account.

Now if we approach this plan in reverse it now feels that same way. If we automatically deposit ALL of our wages into the margin account and buy dividend-bearing stocks right away, this asset becomes our stash. The "bank" becomes our life account.

As we are reluctant to "take money away" from ourselves, it actually will now feel scary to take money OUT of the bank for monthly expenses. We will naturally want to minimize our withdrawals as it feels like we are reducing our fortune, and running up our margin debt.

This reversal of cash flow forces us to be thrifty with our spending. It forces us to consciously pay attention to where our day to day money is going as we have no money in our checking account and we have set up only a monthly or periodic transfer of a pre determined amount.

Here is a snippet of a spreadsheet I created that makes the following assumptions:

1. You start with $20,000.00 in the account (Its OK to start with ZERO, the math still works)
2. You buy a stock worth $25
3. Your monthly dividend is $0.12 per share
4. You Deposit $10,000.00 per month
5. You borrow $6,000.00 per month to live on.

The margin percentage is the $6000 plus interest, minus the dividends. We are just letting the dividends pay down the margin amount owing every month. It seems like it will take a really long time at first.

The account balance goes up by $10,000 a month. This is just a fictional amount to represent you and your partner's total take home pay every month. I know that may seem like a lot to most people but I was just trying to use a nice round number. The math works no matter how much you put in. The magic is in how much you take out, and what dividend yields you can achieve. As you can see, the Margin percentage goes up every month. This can seem scary at first as that percentage grows really fast. Over time, however, it starts to slow down and then reverse as your dividends catch up to and eventually pass the amount of your monthly withdrawals:

Account Balance	# of Shares	Dividends	Margin	Margin Interest	Margin %
$270,000.00	10800	$1296.00	$141124.29	$640.94	52.27%
$280,000.00	11200	$1344.00	$146469.23	$665.21	52.31%
$290,000.00	11600	$1392.00	$151790.44	$689.38	52.34%
$300,000.00	12000	$1440.00	$157087.82	$713.44	52.36%
$310,000.00	12400	$1488.00	$162361.26	$737.39	52.37%
$320,000.00	12800	$1536.00	$167610.66	$761.23	52.38%
$330,000.00	13200	$1584.00	$172835.89	$784.96	52.37%
$340,000.00	13600	$1632.00	$178036.85	$808.58	52.36%
$350,000.00	14000	$1680.00	$183213.43	$832.09	52.35%
$360,000.00	14400	$1728.00	$188365.53	$855.49	52.32%
$370,000.00	14800	$1776.00	$193493.02	$878.78	52.30%
$380,000.00	15200	$1824.00	$198595.80	$901.96	52.26%

The margin percentage peaks at 52.38% then starts to fall as the dividend amount starts to pay it down.

When you visualize this with a chart over 20 years you can see that eventually the dividends will pay back ALL of your margin and also cover your monthly withdrawals.

Depending on the numbers you use you will get different totals and a different time frame, but the curve will be the same:

BYOB

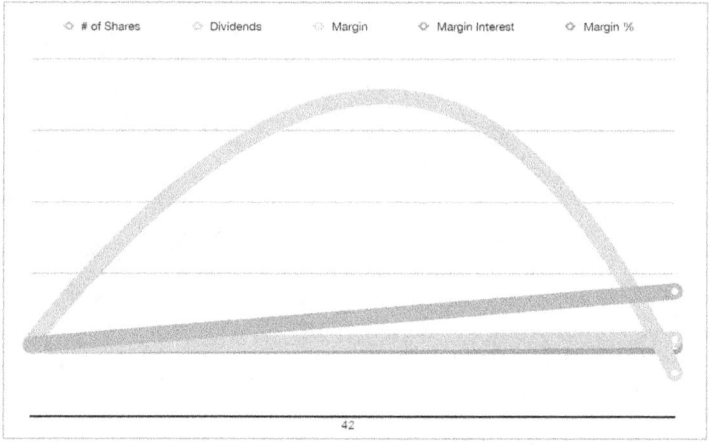

The money in our margin account will grow so fast, we will be amazed. Imagine your yearly salary (and that of your partner) ALL being invested and creating dividend cash flow. We will be completely living off of passive income. Even though we are borrowing at first, the debt is being repaid with dividends so we never spend another cent that we exchanged our precious time for. It is all from the bank. We become bank employees. We are living off an "allowance" from the family fortune while contributing ALL of our money back into the family trust. This sets us up to be just like the blue-blooded families that seem to never run out of money.

YourBank will grow, and you will have freedom and flexibility due to the power of leverage. You will have choice. You will have passive income for the rest of your life.

AFTERWORD

You have now been given a tool. How you choose to use this tool is up to you. You can use it wisely, or you can abuse it. As with all tools, there is great potential to get something done, or to break stuff. I hope I have given you enough information to see the potential of building your fortune this way. You may choose to do it exactly the way I have presented it to you, or you may modify according to your own strategy. I am humbly offering a suggestion. I think this is how you can build and keep wealth for generations. Most fortunes are gone within three generations. This is a statistical fact. I believe the difference in preserving wealth and squandering wealth is your philosophy. Make the family money more important than any one persons' agenda. Commit to the greater good. It is these principles that will be the difference between trading your time for money for 45 years or truly being free.

I have read many books over the years about real estate investing. It seemed to me they had an advantage when it came to building wealth. They had tools and mechanisms written about that were so useful and powerful. I was

Afterword

envious of their ability to use leverage and rental income to perpetuate their cash flow. I wanted to do it too, but life got in the way, and saving up for a down payment seems next to impossible. I had a family to raise, and bills to pay. How can a guy with limited means get into this very cool world? Who has time to manage tenants and fix toilets?

Finding out how to use these same strategies in a different context changed my life. I could use leverage and passive income in the exact same way, and do it with the little money I had. I could play with the big boys! It gave me fuel to chase bigger and better financial dreams and believe that wealth was possible, even for a regular guy like me.

This idea has changed my life. Every time I sit someone down and tell him or her about it, I am blown away by how excited they get. They see the possibilities too and usually can't wait to get started. Most have a margin account opened within a few days. I love seeing the hope in their eyes. I love hearing the plans they have for the income. This is very rewarding for me, and I am so very pleased to be able to share this idea in this book you are reading right now.

If you enjoyed this book and found value in its pages, please take a few moments and leave a review as that will help others find it and benefit from its ideas.

Thank you.

ABOUT THE AUTHOR

Peri Scott is an average guy who became obsessed with the art of money management and passive income. This book is the result of his obsession. Peri has been a professional musician, an investor and a telecommunications executive. He is now proudly the "President and CEO of *ScottBank*". He lives with his family in Canada.

Sign up for our newsletter and enjoy more ideas at: www.beyourownbank.ca

www.ingramcontent.com/pod-product-compliance
Lightning Source LLC
Chambersburg PA
CBHW070430180526
45158CB00017B/962